CHASING THE LION

OVERCOMING DISCOURAGEMENT

GARY SNOWZELL

Published by Freedom Church, a registered charity in England and Wales
(1161926)

CONTENTS

1

LOST ON THE WAY

Recently, my wife Heather and I visited Costa Rica. We had the choice between staying on the Pacific coast or the more desolate Caribbean coast, you know, less tourists, a bit more wild. To anyone who knows me, it'll be no surprise that my first thought was, 'Let's go on an adventure!' It had to be the Caribbean coast.

When we got there we collected our pre-booked 4x4. I had images of us rolling through the island in this all-terrain beast. Instead it turned out to be more of a Fiat Panda with the power of a lawnmower. Despite the disappointment, we set off with renewed excitement through the volcanic misty mountains. The scenery was incredible. The adventure was getting going. But as we rolled up to the higher parts of the mountains we hit endless traffic jams in the remote, high-altitude terrain. 'Where did all these people come from?' we asked ourselves. Here we were in the middle of these tropical mountains and we just couldn't move for traffic. Our sat nav had told us that the journey would take 3.5 hours, luring us into this false sense of security. Instead we went on to encounter some of the craziest traffic delays we have ever experienced.

Where was my jungle paradise?

I was expecting a lush mountain rainforest drive, breathtaking views and nature, you know, that once-in-a-life-time kind of drive. Instead I was being choked by the fumes of more lorries than I had ever seen in one place on the earth. Where was my jungle paradise? Minute by minute the time on that cynical sat nav kept retreating like a game of catch me if you can. We were now 6 hours on a lonely road late at night, in a land far away, just wanting to find our Airbnb.

Driving along we stumbled on a remote beach bar. This was not some tourist wine bar where they hand out maps to your room and offer to take your bags. It was the middle of nowhere, the daylight was fading, and we'd been driving for hours. I reluctantly left the safety of my Fiat Panda to approach the rather interesting, cartel-style bar staff. Amongst some strange smells, I boldly (but poorly) attempted some Spanish to get some help in finding our address. Thankfully, God stepped in, and we miraculously found our jungle tree house after 7 hours on the road. It was far from the arrival I had dreamt up. We crashed inside our tin-roof home whilst I silently questioned, 'What was I thinking?!'

It's very hard to explain the noises of the jungle at night unless you've stayed there. I'd heard people talk about it, but until you experience it you'll never quite get the sound of scraping, tapping, and screeching all over the house. The tin roof amplified every drop of water like it was a bucket load. Exhausted by the drive, you'd think we'd sleep, but it was the total opposite; our eyes were wide open in that pitch black bedroom.The next night it got worse. We experienced the worst weather of the year, as tropical storms battered our tree house whilst limbs of huge trees crashed around us. I was thinking, 'This is not what I expected!'

Then there was the wildlife. Amongst the huge arrival of creepy insects to lovingly join us on our adventure, a marvellous green and black frog popped out. Though fascinated by small creatures, I somehow resisted the urge to pick it up and instead took a photograph for my grandson Nathan. That's when I discovered it was the very deadly poison dart frog! This little beauty packs enough punch to kill you in 10 minutes if the poison gets into your bloodstream. In the middle of nowhere with traffic from hell, we'd have never gotten to a hospital; thank you Lord for saving me! You know we laugh about it now. I wouldn't want to change it, but it was far from what I imagined, a million miles from my expectations.

THE GREAT ADVERSARY

As HUMAN BEINGS we are all subject to expectations: big, small, unreasonable, or unhelpful. Expectations form real estate within our minds, a place our presumptions take us to, that when not met we can sometimes struggle to recover from. Each of us can remember the impact of unmet expectations somewhere in our past. The gap between what we expected would happen and what we actually experienced can form a huge chasm with which we often struggle to reconcile. Without realising it, this can impact our future and our attitude and contain us rather than release us.

I believe that what I'm about to share with you has the potential to change your life. It has the ability to set you free and help you be more prepared to handle whatever comes next. But it starts with self-leadership and that starts with renovating your thinking. In fact unless we take responsibility for challenging the way we think, we will never live the life God called us for.

. . .

DISCOURAGEMENT

In order to renovate your thinking you have to face up to something. You have to deal with the internal and spiritual adversaries that attack your confidence and identity. Dealing with unmet expectations is all about dealing with the greatest adversary of all: discouragement. It's something that comes from within us, around us, and even through the devil himself. The solution is not an overnight quick-fix. It's something that has taken Heather and I over 30 years to understand, but when you get free I can't quite do justice to how liberating that is.

Discouragement impacts us all, and none of us can avoid it. Discouragement knows how to attack you at your lowest point, your place of weakness. It shows no mercy and thrives in your loneliness. Its primary objective is to get you to give up. Discouragement will come at midnight, when you are trying to sleep. That's where it uses unreasonable thoughts to torment you and will start to question you with the dreaded stream of what-ifs. I know many brave people, lionhearts in the Kingdom, and we so often talk about vision and courage and seeing the world change. But as the church, we don't always do a great job of preparing God's people in knowing how the enemy attacks us and even how we attack ourselves. I think there's something here to expose and to grow in for the sake of our future and all we represent.

You see, if the enemy can undermine and remove the courage that God wants to grow within you and replace it with limiting and painful discouragement, then he can alter the life you live. We cannot avoid the giants of discouragement. They wait for us all. But even though we can't avoid them, we do have a choice. We can either run away or we can run down to the battle and face them.

Running down to the battle line sounds exciting to some, but if we do that with the wrong preparation, the wrong perspective, we are unequipped and become overwhelmed. When David ran down to Goliath he didn't wear Saul's armour or take a sword. He took a sling with a handful of stones. It didn't look like much, but what God had done in his heart was so much more powerful than any weapon in his hands. The great news is that there is a way to prepare ourselves so we can disempower discouragement and go on to overcome.

———

QUIT OR GET GOING

WE ALL FACE discouragement in different ways, and its impact is often unique to us individually. My weakness within discouragement is different than yours, and Heather's is different than mine. We're all uniquely wired, and the enemy is a specialist at aiming his shots. He's clever, and he's been practising this for thousands of years. He knows exactly how to come and discourage you. It might be something someone says, or maybe the way they say it. Others don't even notice it, but wow, it just goes deep for you. Often it comes through situations where you're somehow let down. Each situation alone is small, but compounded they break your back. Discouragement comes to remove hope and to wound your heart so that something within you says, 'I just need to give up now.'

The ultimate goal of the discourager is to stop you from moving forward until you feel like quitting is your only option. 'Why keep trying?' It happens everywhere in our lives, even in prayer. I'm sure some of us have prayed and not seen the answers we had hoped for, so we became discouraged and we stepped back. That's why some of us aren't praying as much as we should. Discouragement came in and made us believe we should quit. Some of us were great evangelists, and when we first got saved we'd reach anyone who was around us with the good news of the gospel. But now we step back because we tried with so many people, but they weren't really interested. In fact some just threw it in our face. We felt alienated. Maybe we had one or two friends that responded, and they came along for a few months and then walked away...

I could go on and on because there's going to be a different story for every one of us. But here's the great thing; God has a vision for every one of our lives. His vision for your life is bigger than you can imagine. It is one of liberty and freedom. It is a life unhindered by the sting of unmet expectations, a life of dreams and adventure, a life where you work with Him in seeing the Kingdom come and lives transformed, a life of hope not disappointment.

As CHRISTIANS we like to talk about vision, but we don't always understand how it works. We know we need it, but we don't always see it because vision works on momentum. Once your vision gets momentum it's very hard to stop it, just like once you start rolling a vehicle it's very hard to stop the tonnage. The difficult thing is getting it moving in the first place. The enemy sees the potential within your life, and he will put obstacles under the wheels of your vision so you can't even get moving. You find yourself pushing and thinking, 'Why isn't this going anywhere? Why aren't I seeing results?' He's there with his foot under the wheel doing all he can to stop your momentum from getting started because once it gets going you might start believing this could really work. It might just shift a little bit, maybe just a centimetre, but if you get a sense of movement in your life, if you get a sense of the momentum that you are believing God for, you might start believing for even more. That faith is what disturbs the enemy most of all. His tactic to remove it from our hearts is to attack our vision. There are people reading this right now who have limited your vision because of the discouragement you've experienced in the past. In fact, you have fenced that vision in, and there's a caution in your heart connected to that vision now. You're not putting your whole shoulder into it. You're not fully committed to it. You're no longer devoted to the vision. Discouragement stole your momentum.

But what are you going to do now?

Stay here?

Quit?

There's still courage in you. It might be a dim ember, but it's there!

Get up. Let's get going.

4

DREAMERS AND DUNGEONS

As we read through Genesis, we are introduced to this man Joseph. It can be easy to forget that his life was real. His experience with God was so extraordinary that sometimes it's hard to take in. But Joseph was a real person, a figure in history, who faced disappointment and discouragement just like any of us. Actually, let's be honest, more than most of us, and yet through his life God writes this story of breakthrough and hope. First let's zoom in to meet a 17-year-old Joseph.

A DREAMER

As one of 12 brothers, things are going pretty well because he's a bit of a favourite in the family. His father seems to value him more than his other sons, and he's a dreamer; life is looking good for Joseph. Filled with dreams and vision for the future, he makes the mistake of telling his brothers about his dream that showed them all bowing to him. It did not go down very well. They are offended by it, and they plot to kill him.

Do you know every one of us who are born of Jesus, are dreamers? Joseph is a picture of Jesus, an Old Testament reflection of the Messiah to come. You're a dreamer too, made in His image. Dreams are linked to vision. I wonder if you've ever had a moment like Joseph, speaking out in faith only to be shot down even by those closest to you?

The situation escalates quickly, and this dreamer is soon to be dead. When they get hold of him, some of the brothers have a moment of mercy, so instead of killing him they put him in a pit. It's not as bad as it could have been, but still a pretty bad day for Joseph. There's no going back now though. They can't let him go home, but killing him is a bit too far. Instead they think, 'Why don't we sell him into slavery?' Now it's a real down day.

All of this represents our lives. Joseph was journeying along, and things started off well. He had a great dream, a great vision from God. You had a great vision. God gave you a great dream, and then suddenly someone misunderstood you, somehow something happened, and it felt like you ended up in the pit. A pit of despair where things don't get better, they get worse. Joseph was sold into slavery and taken to Egypt.

Ever felt like you've ended up somewhere foreign? Not foreign to where you live, but just outside of what you planned for your life? Or even outside of what you thought God planned for your life? Maybe where you are right now is not home? Or not where you should be?

Ironically though, things aren't all that bad for Joseph as he arrives in Egypt. He doesn't just get sold into a cheap place, he gets sold into Potiphar's house. This ruler is like a knight, so it's a pretty cushy job. Once again in the rollercoaster life of Joseph, things are looking up. From the despair of the pit it's quickly looking pretty good. On top of this, he has this incredible favour; whatever he does it just seems to turn to success. This favour in his life means he's entrusted with authority and recognised in leadership in the household – an incredible turn around.

THE DUNGEON

Soon though, Potiphar's wife takes a fancy to him; she wants to get her hands on him. She sets him up to fail, offering herself to him, but Joseph stands tall. Even in the craziness of the last season he stays true to God. She grabs his coat as he runs out of there and is so mad about how that looks that she thinks, 'I'm going to accuse him.' She makes her claim to Potiphar, so despite never doing anything wrong, Joseph is put into prison. The dreamer is in the dungeon.

You see it's something the enemy has done to God's people from the beginning. He will accuse you too in an attempt to stop your progress. So often he wants to lock you up in things that aren't even true. It's one of the ways he can stunt the vision for your life.

Again there's something different about Joseph though, and as far as it is possible, prison seems to go well, even without him being looked after. He gets left alone to serve his time, and makes important connections, meeting other prisoners who would have a big part to play in his future. So there's favour coming back into his life, even in the prison. He interprets some dreams of the men around him and says to one of the guys, 'You just remember me when you come before the king." That moment of hope comes again, but then years go by. Joseph remains in prison. Forgotten.

You can imagine the thought process. We're talking of years here. 'God where are you in all of this? Where are you in my despair? What about the promise that seems so delayed?'

DELIVERANCE

It seems like Joseph has to just accept his lot when suddenly one day, he's remembered again. He is brought before Pharaoh, the ruler of the land. In a moment his rollercoaster life is at a pivotal point once again. He interprets the dream that no one else can, finds favour, and is given the position of second-in-command in Egypt. What is this life? The dreamer to the pit, the pit to palace, the palace to the dungeon, and now with more authority than anyone else except Pharaoh? The story isn't full circle yet though. Some time later his family arrive, the same brothers whose anger and jealousy had started this crazy journey decades ago. They don't recognise him. His brothers bow before him and ask for help. The dream that got him into all that trouble is fulfilled.

5

REALITY CHECK

WITHIN THE CHURCH we love to preach blessing. We preach about what we're going to believe for and how we're going to see the promises of God fulfilled. We preach about how we're going to see healing and provision, and that's not a bad thing. However, we tend to focus on the ups, and we don't always talk about the downs. In reality, our journey to the fullness of God's calling and promise can have significant challenges or delays. Joseph's story is such a reality check for us. You see, when the dream first landed in Joseph's life he was 17. When he was reconciled to his family and the vision fulfilled, Joseph was 41. That's 24 years. Let that sink in, 24 years! The problem is that when we only focus on the blessing or promise, it can create in us a false sense of what the journey will look like. We think it'll take '3.5 hours' and be scenic and beautiful. When we get stuck in the traffic or the detours or the delays we doubt, we question, and we can even give up on the destination. I believe we need to learn how to handle the journey. We need to learn how to handle disappointment and discouragement because if we don't learn to handle it, we will never make it to our moments of deliverance. When I look at Joseph's life it's easy to imagine how this 17-year-old boy could have become angry and resentful. He could have remained in a pit of bitterness his whole life, but he didn't. He could have allowed one moment to define or derail the rest of what God was doing, but he didn't.

Let's be honest though, he must have struggled at points. Imagine the feelings and thoughts that would have plagued him in those moments alone and forgotten. So many of us today are led by our feelings and emotions, but Joseph's endurance could not have come from a feeling alone. Instead he made choices to stay focused and trust that what God had said would come to pass. We are all faced with those same choices every day. Will we become bitter or move forward towards better? Will we give up when the journey takes longer than we expected? Will we choose a safer detour just so we don't have to keep driving through the night seasons in our lives? I don't want to see believers and leaders having a great start, only to experience a bit of burnout and discouragement, and then end up disappearing from the field. I want to see you get through to the end and finish well. Heather and I know this journey well, and I wish we were told this at the start. Most people only see where we are today: building church on 4 continents and seeing people receive Jesus each week. The reality is that when Heather and I started church in our early 20s with a team of 6 we did not have a clue what we were doing.

· · ·

RECENTLY, when we celebrated 13 decisions to follow Christ in one of our new church plants in Cambodia, it was such a reality check of those early days. The church there had only been going for six weeks; it took us six years to see that number of salvations when we first started. 'Maybe we needed more faith,' some would say, but it wasn't because we didn't believe. We believed every week with every invite we gave out and every outreach event we ran. We didn't lack passion or faith for what God could do, and even though the early years were difficult, we did slowly begin to see things happen. We saw provision, miracles, and answers to our prayers, but then suddenly, one of our church planters contracted cancer. When there are only six people in your team and one of you is dying, you're in a pit. We'd stepped out, we were trusting God, how on earth was this part of the plan? We all believed, with all our hearts, with all our faith. We fought for her. She was family. We were by her bed just before she died. We were there when she worshipped God as she went to glory, but well before old age we lost her.

I remember having to do the funeral. What was I meant to say to the team I'm leading, the family that had lost a loved one? Where do we go from here? Thrown into this place of loss and confusion, we were facing a decision: to go on believing or to give up and stay? This was us in the pit. In the coming season, people left the church as well. Even some of our original team went separate ways. Here we were dealing with loss, and now the pain of not doing church with people we thought we'd build with forever is added to it.

Slowly, we got our courage up again. We remembered to trust. We surrendered needing to understand it all, and we kept building church. Amazingly, we saw miraculous provision for a building; God came through for us almost out of nowhere. Our courage shot up. We were feeling undefeatable once again, we were back on track. Next, however, the challenge would come in our own lives.

6

PERSONAL PRISON

HEATHER and I are so passionate about reaching people and building the church. In the early years, we had very little money as a church, and anything we had we wanted to use to reach people rather than as wages for ourselves. But we needed to find a way of putting food on the table for our family, so I had to run a business.

Over the years, we tried several different things, including a pet shop at one time. Most of the businesses failed, but others began to work and provide for us. 7 years into the process of hard work and sacrifice, things were going ok, and we just about had our head above water. Then someone we were in business with went bankrupt without warning, and it plunged us into huge debt. We almost lost everything we had. With 4 young children, a church to lead, and now a struggling business, I was overwhelmed with feelings of failure and had no quick solution to sort it. Was this part of the plan? Where's the miraculous provision this time? It wasn't even our debt in the first place, but rather something we inherited because of other people's business decisions.

It took us five years to recover from that debt. Those five years felt like a prison for me. The up of the miraculous breakthrough for a building was now contrasted by this debt that wasn't even our fault. Every month we were believing, working every hour we could just to keep up the payments, and man were we praying. We believed for a shift; we believed for a supernatural breakthrough. Instead, God had us walk through that season step by step; there was no short-cut. I remember God saying to me, 'There's no quick escape, but will you trust me in this?' And it wasn't just about finding a way through financially. Getting up every week as a pastor and bringing God's word when this was going on in the background was a huge challenge, as was raising our sons when I felt like a failure. Life was a constant blur of ups and downs. There were many other challenges that we were going through as well, leaving us feeling overwhelmed by the situations we found ourselves in. I remember God asking me, 'Are you going to get your head up when you get up and preach every week? Will your family see you marked by discouragement or faith?' I was faced daily with a decision. I could choose to live in the fruit of discouragement as a victim and become bitter, or I could choose to learn through this and become better. At times we were exhausted by disappointment and our spirits were heavy, but we always felt God lifting our heads. The Holy Spirit constantly reminded us that even in the disappointment it was a time to engage with him, a time to keep pushing through.

I connect to the story of Joseph because, although I haven't actually been in a physical prison, I've been in a spiritual prison, which I had to endure before I could break out. As I cried out to God to deliver me, I found myself in a place where God said, 'You've got a few years here because I will do something here that can't be done anywhere else.' There are things that will be done in the dark that you can't get done anywhere else. These are the things that we must visit the pit and prison seasons to develop.

WE CAME THROUGH THE DEBT, and after some hopeful, fruitful years, the church was starting to really move in an exciting direction. We'd crossed over into a new larger city. We were seeing an influx of families and young people, and there was a sense of expectation and opportunity in everything. Then we were hit with one of the toughest things we'd faced so far.

Heather's mum was suddenly taken ill, and it went from a general hospitalisation to a life threatening situation in just a couple of days. Very shortly after, she died. We were in total shock. She went from being full of life to no longer with us long before she should have. Whilst we were still dealing with the shock and grieving from the tragic loss, we found out that Heather's dad was unwell with Alzheimer's. Heather's mum had been coping with it, but now that she'd gone, his condition became more and more apparent. Over the next few years the family helped care for him until he went into a nursing home and eventually died of cancer. All this time we were building Freedom Church, raising our 5 boys, and these things were happening in our lives too. Many people wouldn't know about a lot of the pain and the grief we experienced because we chose not to give up. We still had people to lead and love. I still had to find that message to bring each week.

We chose to celebrate and continue to declare the promises of God, always believing the best was yet to come. It was like we knew that there were others who were waiting for us, unknown people yet to be awoken, to be rescued, to be restored. There were marriages to be made, children to be born, and, yes, nations to be changed. This is what caused us to stare down discouragement and refuse to give up. You might be struggling through this valley of discouragement, but you've got to keep pushing. Change is coming. Don't give up. God wants to make you stormproof: someone who will make it through to the end well, not someone who complains and gives up at the first sign of resistance. You don't realise how much you have within you, but it is a power that conquered the grave, a power that can get you through this season.

WE'RE at an amazing point in our life right now, seeing so much fruitfulness after those barren years, but I do not take this for granted. I can't presume that we've made it, or that we're through the trials. We are still in the middle of our ministry, and I'm fully aware that anything can happen. Whatever is ahead is going to take more, but at least now we understand in a greater way that the detours, delays, and challenges shape us as we journey. When Heather lost her mum and dad so close and so early, it put a resilience into her. It absolutely broke her heart, but there's another level of strength in her now. I remember some time after the loss, Heather saying to me, 'I realise now that I spent years being upset by things that didn't really matter, others opinions and disappointments, which were not worth my time. So I have decided, I won't ever cry over things that don't really matter in this life anymore.' True to her word, Heather changed. Not by becoming hardened, she still is one of the most compassionate people I know and is moved to tears for the right reasons, but now she has developed a resilience and character which has made her stormproof.

7

EXPECTATIONS - THE JOURNEY

So HOW DO we do it? Well, I believe that it is connected to our expectations. In fact I believe that if we don't learn to manage our expectations the right way, then we will spend a lifetime dealing with the crippling effects of discouragement or disappointment. There's a huge problem in the church, and in all of humanity, because you and I place too much of our peace on our expectations being met in specific ways. You may think I'm speaking a bit negatively, but stay with me because I want to be real with you. We have all fallen into the trap of believing that if we are good Christians: tithing and volunteering, helping others, and perhaps leading in some way, then surely things in our lives should be slotting into place, right? When it doesn't happen we start thinking there's something wrong with us. Many of us have received the dream, the prophecy, and the calling, but we never stopped to consider the hardship, rejection, and delay that was all part of the plan too.

Expectation is everything. We taught the promise, but we didn't teach the risk. We learnt that we are overcomers, but we didn't teach about the battle. We have raised people who think that if they have prayed for it and claimed it, then they deserve it. However, that's not always the route to the destination. Sometimes there's another way, maybe a delay and maybe a fight, where standing firm is all you can do.

Unmanaged expectations will create a false perspective, and then we so easily combine our discouragements across all areas of our life. We can start making comparisons with that person in the next row who is getting all the answers to prayer. He's got the job, got the girl, got the life; he's got it all! But let me tell you that you don't know what it may have cost him. You don't know the dark times he faced but decided to keep standing. We are in a fruitful time now, and some people will judge, presuming that we've had it easy, but they don't know the price we paid. We often don't realise that God is doing a deep renovation work within us. It's an excavation that is not short-term. When you build on the rock you've got to be ready to go deep. If we just focus on the high points, looking for the next experience to flatter us, the next prophetic word to make us feel invincible, we could be easily disappointed. When we live a life determined by feelings, we build on the sand, which is inconsistent and unreliable.

HERE's the other trick of the enemy though too: when discouragement settles in, it paralyses our heart so that we begin to lower our expectations. It comes full circle, and we withdraw from praying the faith-filled prayers we once prayed. We play it safe, and we learn to live smaller than we should. Over time, our disappointments turn to resentment, and then resentment can turn to depression. We can blame our condition on the fruit of the circumstances we've gone through, but we have to reverse right up and come back to the root. We need to look at the cause and not the effect to realise that some of our lives are continually controlled by unmet expectations that may not even be rooted in reality. We can feel like changing the world on a Sunday, but as soon as we have bad news or hit disappointment on a Monday we are feeling like the world is against us. It's a bit like Humpty Dumpty; when we're up, we're up and when we're down, we're really down. This was never the life that Christ called us to live. He called us to be free in the storm.

I'm sure I'm speaking to some pastors here, some leaders. You have been praying for and ministering to someone, but as soon as you deal with one problem it's not long before they're coming with another; it's exhausting. You're planning yet another counselling session or ministry night, hoping it will do the trick. But we all have to play our part in digging ourselves out of the pit we're in instead of just looking to others to do it for us. You will find your biggest ladder to climb out of every pit is around this whole area of your expectations.

I cannot control what will happen tomorrow, but I can take responsibility for my expectations. The choice is ours. You can quote all the scripture you want, my friend. You can be at every prayer meeting, you can receive the most amazing words, you can be in the presence, or connect to your favorite preacher through a podcast for the best word ever, but if you don't learn to manage expectations, you'll spend a lifetime managing discouragement.

We used to allow unmanaged, unmet expectations to dominate our life. Our expectations were based on presumption and a sense of entitlement towards our vision becoming fulfilled. We had inherited a pattern of thinking about how to see something happen. Firstly, we were going to declare it through prayer, then we were going to believe for the answer, then finally, we were going to act as if it had already been answered. Following that process when our answer didn't happen left us confused and very discouraged. What did we do wrong? I remember going for walks for hours, asking God to tell me if there was some hidden sin that was getting in the way of my request? Or maybe I'm too distracted? Perhaps I'm not sacrificing enough? There I was on my knees, asking the Lord to purge me or reveal some blind spot I couldn't see. Finally, I realised that all of my disappointment was caused by assumptions I'd made, not times I had failed. I suddenly started waking up to the fact that I had to manage my expectations without reducing my faith.

I was drawn to the story of Jonathan and His armour bearer. They went on a 'do or die' mission, and Jonathan began his Braveheart speech in 1 Samuel 14 by declaring, '*Perhaps* the Lord will help us, for there is nothing to prevent the Lord from saving, whether by many or by few.' He wasn't going with an expectation of any guaranteed victory or success. He was confessing, 'I'm not entirely sure, and I'm certainly not entitled, but what I do have is an opportunity and just *perhaps* God will move for us'. There it is; amazing faith, under managed expectation, followed up by courageous action.

———

8

EXPECTATIONS - PEOPLE

I LOOK BACK through my years as a leader and see many casualties throughout the journey. Some of those had responded to the call to go church planting only to discover the journey was too demanding, leaving them battle-scarred and unhealthy. They started out presuming that in their response to the call, they would live the dream that they felt entitled to because of their sacrifice. They soon found that they didn't arrive at the palace. Maybe we didn't do a good enough job of preparing them. We certainly spoke about faith and vision and expectation, but we didn't tell them about the pit. This saddens my heart. There is a part of me that continues to grieve for those that responded, those who left family and went, people that had an expectation, but walked away when it wasn't fulfilled, often into a worse place. I'm not talking about people who moved on into a new healthy season; I'm talking about those that got up and, through unmet expectations, became strangled by resentment. Bitterness caused them to walk away into a prison. If that's you, I continually pray for you, and I want you to know that the door is not locked. No one can lock the door to the dream that God gave you.

WE PLACE so much expectation upon those who lead us as well. The bible clearly teaches us that leaders have a great responsibility, but so often we place an expectation upon them that no human being can achieve. I have lost count of the times, especially in our early years, when we were pastoring people who we helped, supported, gave all that we could for, only for them to come and say 'I'm so disappointed in you Pastor, I just feel you let me down.' Many people will feel like you should have known, you should have asked, and you should have done more to help them. I could tell story after story of things like, 'If you were more of a caring Church", 'If you were more the way that Jesus called you to be', 'If we had better pastors, we wouldn't be in the bad place we are in now.' I used to believe it, and I would question if I might be the worst, most dysfunctional pastor and if I should resign. One of the statements that used to sting was, 'I know a lot of other people feel like this as well, Pastor.' The problem was when I started asking who else feels like this, most of the time they would reluctantly name one or two other people and rarely be able to quantify their complaint. I'm not saying there may not have been things we could have done better, but so often failed expectations have this habit of inflating situations, blaming others, and not taking personal responsibility.

I've realised that I could be the most incredible, flawless leader, but I'll still let someone down. I want to remind you how careful you've got to be with how much expectation you put upon those who lead you, including your pastor. I have often challenged my own leaders that, although I may be the Senior Pastor of Freedom Church, I am very human, I make mistakes, and if I was to fail I wouldn't want anyone to give up this fight on account of my failure. If you did give up, it would be because you had an unreal expectation of me that maybe somehow I'm perfect. But life shows us that we are all on our journey to Jesus. I am not perfect. The amazing team I work with are not perfect. So let's stop putting that on them. We're all in this together; we're journeying this together. We don't always know what others are going through, and we can't always understand the weight which comes from leading people.

Leaders, maybe you have experienced this. You have done all you can to lead, encourage, help, and disciple the people under your care. Then it comes to light that they don't feel you did enough. They criticise or walk away. Here's my advice: don't be surprised, but just get over it and carry on. Learn what you need to learn, change, but keep moving forward. Jesus didn't say, 'They're all going to think you're wonderful.' We were never promised an easy ride or full agreement without conflict. You're just going to have to decide who you're doing it all for. It's too tempting to get caught up in people's opinions, but we are doing this for the King. We don't realise that the church is like a bus. People get on, and they get off. Don't worry when people leave. If I tried to keep everyone on the bus, it wouldn't be any good, and honestly, sometimes we need some people to get off.

Unwilling people, reluctant people, and unchanging people can choke the life out of vision.

As I've led our church in key transition seasons, every now and then I would slow down to encourage the people who need to get off. I did this intentionally for a couple of years when I began to understand the truth around expectations. I'm not obliged to win reluctant, negative people anymore. In that season I kept saying, 'Hey, the door is open if you want to move on from this. Now is a great opportunity, maybe this vision isn't for you? Maybe you'll be happy in another church?' After a while of doing this, Heather said, 'I think you've done enough of that now! You keep telling people to leave. Maybe now you need to focus on those who have actually decided to come on the journey...' Heather is my sensitive side. So I took her advice and found the balance.

I now have no expectation about how many people we need or how many churches we should plant before we are deemed a success in the eyes of others. My goal is to be faithful and relentless in this do-or-die mission, without compromise or excuse. I want to always remember whose glory we are doing this for. Simply accepting who He's called us to be and not trying to win the approval of others has been a huge confidence builder. God has called us to carry this vision in our own unique way, for such a time as this. It's incredible; it's liberating.

ONE OF THE most influential areas where expectations matter is around family. We could be here all day if I started talking about family dynamics. You see, we all have an expectation of family, and they have an expectation of us. Unspoken expectations are often what cause our relationships to fracture, and so many live in regret when those expectations are unmet. The hurt which follows has separated many families throughout our world. I had an expectation of my parents when they became grandparents, and it wasn't fulfilled in the way I expected. It led me into a place of disappointment and hurt until I removed my expectation. I have discovered that to maintain a healthy relationship, I need to manage my expectations and what I may feel entitled to as a son. In turn this has released them, and it has protected my heart.

Should we have expectations of people in life then? Of course! God has an expectation of me as a husband, father, and leader. Knowing that drives me and helps me. It's the unmanaged, often unspoken, and unrealistic expectations we place on people that are so dangerous. We need to live in the balance of faith for and in people, at the same as never expecting perfection from them.

What expectations do you have of the people in your life; your spouse, leader or family? What expectations do you have of yourself? What expectations are right, and what do you need to remove? We're all human. We succeed. We fail. Your expectations of those around you, when unmet, can put you in a prison of resentment. Release it. Release them, and release yourself.

9

INSIDE OUT CONSISTENCY

IMAGINE THIS; you've been trying to get a new job, waiting and applying and feeling the financial strain and the frustration of being stuck where you don't want to be. Then you get this one opportunity, like a carrot dangling in front of a donkey. You think, here it comes! You can almost grab it, it's so close. It's just like all those prophetic words you've received. God is good! Amen? Until you reach out to grasp it, and someone else takes it. Or, you actually get what you want, and it's not quite as it appeared. Then you end up wishing someone else had the rotten carrot.

That has happened to me many times. It happened last week, actually. Something I had been working on for over a year, investing time and money into, was just about to come through, and then it was just gone. I have prayed about decisions and stepped out in faith, believing God was with me. I have claimed the favour of the Lord as His son, only for it to end up going completely wrong, costing me time and focus for no rational reason. I could tell you so many stories and some still continue, but where discouragement would have impacted me greatly in the past, I've learnt that I can live a life from the inside out rather than outside in. When life happens, it's down to me to manage those expectations, which allows me to live a life of consistency and not reaction.

With this recent situation, I didn't tell Heather for a couple of days because I didn't want to give it more importance than it actually had. When I finally told her, she had not even been able to tell I had had that bad news because it didn't change my mood. Please understand that I'm not saying, 'Don't have expectations.' I'm encouraging you to believe for impossible things, but manage your expectations around those things. During the last few weeks I have had one disappointment after another, watching things that I hoped for dry up and die. I've realised that these things are designed to distract me by occupying my mind with temporal things so that I take focus off what really matters. Believe me, it's still gutting, and for a moment there is this sinking feeling of discouragement. But instead of spending weeks feeling flat, I've learnt to manage those feelings so that Heather often doesn't even know what I've been dealing with unless I tell her because I'm still making the great jokes that make her laugh. News like that should not change our joy or our decision to always believe God is good all the time. He is faithful, and He will never disappoint.

LIKE MYSELF IN those early days, some of us are great when things are going well in our lives and we are getting what we want, when we want it. We can believe for anything and give advice to those less fortunate. But when things go wrong, when there is loss, and we don't get what we feel we need, when discouragement comes we sulk and we swim in the lake of self pity.

Some of us are bad company because of discouragement. Some of us have always got a list, and we need someone to pray for us. In love, let me tell you that you've had enough prayer for a lifetime, and it's time to start managing your expectations. We can often react by not feeling like attending that prayer meeting, excusing ourselves and claiming some 'me-time'. Soon we're coming up with reasons not to go to small groups, finding ourselves especially irritated by the faith and passion of others. So we hang back, stay in, watch something pathetic on the TV, and go to bed with a troubled mind. We complain to God about the situation for the rest of the week and retreat in isolation to avoid any input that could challenge our attitude. We have got to wake up. We can play the victims for as long as we want, or we can realise that it's all based around our unmanaged expectations.

When we manage expectations, there is a consistency line that is running through our life which causes us to not be reactionary, but rather to take action, no matter what is going on around us. As a lionheart, God has given you the ability to live a consistent life. I've learnt that when you manage expectations your faith increases, and so, your healthy, faith-filled expectations cause a greater consistency as you journey. We cannot let the circumstances we experience determine our peace.

Consistency is far more likely to be achieved when we are getting our strength from inside factors rather than outside ones. I am not saying that we reduce our expectation to reduce disappointment. If anything, our expectation should increase because our consistent faith becomes even more audacious. I have learnt to expect anything.

———————

CONQUER AND MANAGE

As you go forward in life and leadership, managing your expectation is key. I've learnt that there's three main areas that are vital to get this right in. You have to conquer and manage your expectations of yourself, others, and God.

EXPECTATIONS OF YOURSELF

You've got to confront and manage the misplaced expectations you have placed upon yourself before they cripple you. I placed an expectation on myself to be a certain type of Christian for many years and felt like I couldn't achieve it. Other people seemed holier than me, better at praying than me, more knowledgeable than me, and a toxic comparison came into my life. When we see what God is doing in others, we only witness the results. We don't see the cost and all that has gone on underneath the surface. The enemy is so crafty at getting us to criticise our own faith, to look at our doubt. He points out our shortcomings in case we actually believe God may use us. He points out our failures from our past.

For me, he even pointed out and reminded me of the people who left me in order to reinforce the thought that I am not worth following. Every one of us has experienced failure within our lives, and the enemy has this tactic of taking an Instagram picture of your failure to repost again and again in your mind until you feel like you can never move on. But God doesn't take Instagram pictures; He takes video. Your life is a movie, and it's not finished. This is a film in the making. Some of you are too hard on yourselves. Some of you scrutinise and criticise yourselves. God wants you to come to Him, enjoy His presence, and grow in Him. We pressure ourselves, but our Father is inviting you closer because He delights in who you are. He made you, and no one could be a better you. You are enough, so it's time to believe what He says about you rather than what you feel about you.

EXPECTATIONS OF OTHERS

Secondly, you have to deal with your expectations of others. Whether it's leaders, family, friends, or your boss at work, we can set others up to fail and ourselves to be let down because of what we place upon others.

In managing your expectations of others, I'm not talking about ignoring unacceptable behaviour or brushing under the carpet ungodly leadership. I'm certainly not saying anyone should stay in an abusive relationship, for example, just because it's not what you expected. Absolutely not. You have to speak up, speak out, and get out of that situation.

I'm saying, in normal relationships, stop expecting perfection from people. Stop placing on others expectations that if it were expected of you, you'd reject it. Stop allowing the unspoken expectations inside you to judge someone without them even knowing it. In our church we encourage couples who are about to get married to talk about their expectations ahead of their wedding day. We talk about our expectations of each other even though we've been married over 36 years. It's an important discussion to have. Opening up the conversation is one of the ways we manage our expectations, but you have got to be willing to change yours. Release the unrealistic, unspoken expectations, and it will be so liberating.

Strangely, we can even put an expectation on those we're trying to reach as well. We invite people to our church who have no faith, and when they don't come (and even start avoiding us) we get so discouraged. What were you expecting? Again in Matthew 10, Jesus told his followers that they were going to go into communities with this gospel, and it would be rejected by some. Jesus simply says, 'Move on and go somewhere where they are receptive to your message.' He is instructing them to manage their expectations of people. We cannot allow our hopeful projection of people's responses to be our motivation. Whether accepted or rejected, we must keep doing what we were called to do.

EXPECTATIONS OF GOD

This is a big one because we all have formed our own expectations of God, and we feel entitled to the fulfilment of those expectations. We have given them rights through our toxic religion and poor theology, and if God doesn't line up with what we hold in our minds we feel let down by Him. We distance ourselves like spoiled children not getting their way. Many of us think He's like a vending machine; if you pray enough, give enough, volunteer enough, and sacrifice enough, then He should definitely come through for you because doesn't he come through for the good people? Bad things surely don't happen to good people, especially not Christians!

Tell John the Baptist that. He had an expectation that Jesus would come save him. After all, Jesus was doing miracles for everyone else. John was related for goodness sake, and not a bad preacher either, so he waited for his miracle. And then Jesus said, I'm not coming! We've got this weird belief that the more we give, the greater our reward will be because you cannot out give God, can you? This wrong expectation is the reason many of us have stopped praying, stopped evangelising, pulled back, and become timid with it, but God is saying it's time to find your roar once again. I believe there's vision yet to be fulfilled for every one of you, but unless you manage your expectation of who God is, it will remain unrealised. When we drift from the solid ground of gratitude and slip into the sands of entitlement, we allow disappointment to paralyse us as we get mad with God.

God is a good father that wants good things for His children; that will always be true. Sometimes that good comes in a way we don't expect or a journey we'd have rather avoided, but it will come. In the cross we already have been given an immense gift of a second chance: life in heaven. Every joy we experience on this earth and every breakthrough we are a part of is a bonus.

As Christians we are waging war against the kingdom of darkness, involved in a cosmic plan, and yet we presume this will be uncontested or untested. But when I signed up for being a radical Jesus-follower, I gave up my rights to preserve my life. So, I have learnt to be prepared and not be surprised by the lies, dirty tricks, and disqualification attempts that the darkness will throw from time to time.

Jesus put it this way in Matthew 10; I'm sending you like lambs to the slaughter, or even lambs to wolves. It doesn't really get much worse than that! In preparing the disciples, Jesus wanted to get their expectations managed. He wants them to know that it could get a bit messy, but do you know what you need to celebrate? That your names are written in the book of life! You need to celebrate that this is the eternal treasure. He has a plan for the most inconsistent person I'm talking to, the one who is bullied by that enemy discouragement. This is God's guerrilla warfare to bring stability into your life, and it's based upon being faithful.

Wherever you feel that God has 'let you down', change your perspective. Walk out of that place, live a life of consistency, and take responsibility for your expectations. Start to say, 'God, you're good, no matter what happens tomorrow. You're good, no matter if I get that job. You're good, no matter if I go to prison. You're good.' That's what brings the freedom of the lionheart. The unfailing truth of God's goodness and the power of our faith to follow are what will take us to the places that God has ahead of us.

11

FINISH WELL

WITH EACH HEARTBREAKING LOSS, we had a choice to stay in the pit or to manage our expectations. We believed, nevertheless, that God is good, and He is kind, and we can either choose to live as daring dreamers or stagnate in our discouragement and hurt. This is what we learnt. We committed to manage our expectations according to God's truth, not our feelings, in order to fulfil the potential of the dreams placed inside of us. Those dreams represent others, and everything about advancing the Kingdom involves bringing life and breath to dead bones. That's what gets us up every day. Although there have been and will be casualties, we will bring life to as many souls as we can whilst we have breath.

I sincerely hope every one of you will make it to the finish strong in this faith. I'm cheering you on and believing you will finish well. But if you don't, I'm going to keep going regardless. I say that about my closest friends and family because I can't enter into this with terms and conditions; 'As long as that doesn't happen, as long as my son comes through' and so on. The enemy wants you to make a deal, and he wants to fill you with fear and discouragement. Those you love might end up in a bad place. Sometimes for a season it can look hopeless, but God is asking us to follow with complete trust, hope and faith.

When I question and doubt how good God is, He reminds me of this verse which appears at the very end of Joseph's encounter with his brothers in Genesis 45: 7-8 NIV, 'But God sent me ahead of you to preserve for you a remnant on earth and to save your lives by a great deliverance. So then, it was not you who sent me here, but God. He made me father to Pharaoh, lord of his entire household and ruler of all Egypt.'

God allowed Joseph to experience rejection, the pit, false accusation, prison and loss of freedom, all because he had a plan for a far bigger purpose, more than Joseph could have ever imagined. This is why our lives need to be consistent. We may not understand what the bigger picture is when we're in the pit, but if Joseph hadn't gone into the pit, he would have never ended up in the palace. His rejection led to his direction. We don't want the rejection, and we don't want to be in the pit. We just want to get to the palace. I'm here to tell you, that is part of the course, and we need to be ready with our feet firmly on the ground, shoulder behind the vision, stormproof, and offence-free, pushing forward towards the goal. This is the confidence that we have in Romans 8:28 NIV, 'And we know that in all things God works for the good of those who love him.'

. . .

Don't reduce your faith to a place where you risk less. Have a sustainable faith that cannot be rocked or shaken, a faith that will deal with disappointment and discouragement, a faith that expects more. Don't be a one-hit wonder, but a dreamer like Joseph who was defiant with his faith and was proven through trials. That same chapter in Romans 8:35 AMP says, 'Who shall ever separate us from the love of Christ? Will tribulation, or distress, or persecution, or famine, or nakedness, or danger, or sword?' Can the pit separate me? No, in all these things, pressures, pain, and the problems we encounter, nothing can separate us from His love. Let this speak to your fear and into your discouragement. I pray that prison doors will open in Jesus' name. I believe there are people with discouragement, in their pit, thinking their dreams are dead and it won't change for them. But God wants to remind us that He took the keys and set us free. We just need to walk through this season.

Daring dreamers, you need to manage your expectations today. Expect that God will do a miracle, but understand that it's you that has got to walk it out. God gave you that dream that seems impossible to others, but there's something in you that is daring to believe it could happen. Approach with well-managed expectations. I repeat this to myself almost every week, 'Believe for everything, presume nothing.' I have decided to live my life believing anything is possible with God, but presuming nothing in order to protect my heart and to fight entitlement. We are yet to see the greatest signs and wonders, for surely the best days of the daring dreamers are ahead of us.

ABOUT THE AUTHOR

Gary Snowzell and his wife Heather are the Senior Pastors of Freedom Church, a global church-planting movement based out of the UK. With over 30 years in ministry, Gary writes with a passion for people, the church, and the gospel. Through the highs and lows of life and leadership, Gary has formed a formidable determination to keep going when all is stacked against him. His writing will inspire you, equip you, and transform you.

Printed in Great Britain
by Amazon